But Before You Leave

Kirsten Corley

Dedicated to my friends and family, especially my mom and dad. Without your love and constant support I wouldn't be able to pursue anything.

Special dedication to Nathan Long and Tom Kinsella

To everyone you've ever loved.
To everyone you've ever lost.
And to the precious few who have chosen to stay.

You

This is to every person you've ever loved. All those words you couldn't say. Familiar strangers walking around with empty pockets and broken hearts, unaware that you adore all that they are.

I don't care what the question is. With you the answer will always be yes.

I hope you think of me and the taste of regret leaves your mouth dry and bitter.

It was 2 AM and I was thinking of you. I don't know what greater compliment there is.

Darling, so many people love and care about you, but you're only focused on the one who doesn't.

Try losing the only thing you care about and not going insane. I dare you.

Losing you would be like losing part of me, only it'd be losing the best part of me.

You're always gonna be too much of something. So how about instead of fixating upon what you wish you could change, why don't you change the people you associate with who are making you feel this way?

Even if your voice is shaking, never stop asking for what you want.

That girl cares about you. You'd be a fool for not realizing the value in that.

We all have our own demons we fight late at night. Don't let them destroy you. Don't let them win. Don't let them make you believe you aren't the most miraculous person in the entire world.

Part of me wants to fall into you and trust everything you say. The other part of me is terrified and wants to take off before I get hurt for making such a mistake.

Everything you don't like about yourself, someone is going to adore one day.

Whatever may or may not happen in the future, I find comfort in knowing someone like you even exists in the world.

Even if it's killing you, you gotta pretend it's not. The only way someone can miss you is if they see you're better off without them.

The best advice my dad ever gave me was, "If anyone leaves you confused for even a moment, it means they aren't sure of something in their own life. Walk away because you don't need anyone who isn't 100% sure they want you."

If you have to try that hard, I can guarantee one thing, they probably aren't worth it.

If you don't want to be that girl, then don't be her. But you have to make a decision about whom you want to be and pursue that.

I love you, but you live in your own world sometimes. And I don't quite know what to do about it. You get lost in thoughts and a false reality. And sometimes I want to just pull you back in, but I look at you and I could tell you're worlds away. And I don't know how to get there.

Always remember there isn't ever just gonna be one person who makes your heart skip a beat.

Whatever it is you are recovering from, whether it's heartbreak, an eating disorder, drug addiction, depression, or a suicide attempt. Maybe it's just a bad day. Whatever it is you are going through right now that no one knows about, I want you to know you aren't alone. I want to remind you to keep going. And I want you to trust me when I say it will get better.

If I like you, you should know it's only you. I'll give you my undivided attention. I'll give you my best. I refuse to mess with your head or keep you on your toes. Or play that game. Because to me that isn't fun. To me, fun is looking someone in the eyes and saying, "I want you and only you."

Kind words are never wasted. Vulnerability doesn't make you weak. And those moments someone doesn't say the things you want to hear back make you stronger than you've ever imagined. You just don't see it yet.

"I wish it didn't hurt so much."

"I know you do. But you should know, the people who hurt more, love deeper. And the people who love deeper, love the right way. And the people who love the right way, find love that lasts."

Raw honesty is so rare these days, you thought I was trying to deceive you.

You gotta believe there's something better for you than someone who makes your heart hurt and someone who gives you a halfhearted love story.

And in the midst of ordinary days, sometimes life gets interrupted with fairy tales.

You've been waiting by your phone every night for him to answer. He has answered, in silence. It's just not what you want to hear.

I think one of the hardest things you'll ever have to do is just picking up and getting on with things when you haven't a clue how you got there in the first place.

It's risky and your heart's beating and you wonder, "Am I gonna get hurt?" But you gotta take those kinds of chances; you gotta do the things that scare you because on the other side of fear, pain, and rejection is something magnificent we all hope for.

If someone hurt you or made you cry, the last thing in the world you ever have to say is sorry.

My wish for all of you is to respect yourself enough that you never tolerate mistreatment or pain. It begins with you. You deserve more and I know you know it, too.

It isn't you. I want you to know that some people just aren't ready for a good thing to come into their life. And when that happens, they run because it's unlike anything they've ever known.

Darling, just because someone isn't loving you back doesn't mean you are doing it wrong. It just means they are wrong. Please don't mistake the two.

But if I can remind you of one thing, it's that an individual hurt you, not love.

You have all these ideas of what you wanna do with that person you haven't met yet. Then you meet them and you realize you could watch fucking paint dry and it would still be the greatest thing in the world because you're with the only person that matters.

That moment you get it right, you realize it was supposed to be this whole. Everything else was just noise.

Your heart says don't give up on it, but your head says you should know better. And the greatest question of all is, how do you look at someone you adore and just walk away?

Your name is tattooed on every heart you touch; more than that, it leaves scars on the ones you break.

If you feel it, it's real.

When you walk away with an uncertainty of the next time your paths will cross, "goodbye" becomes the saddest word.

You brought light into a world in which I only knew darkness. And before we parted ways, you painted me this world on the most beautiful easel, reminding me of a place you destroyed.

The dark shadow taking my hand was almost inviting because when you dance with the Devil there is nothing in life to fear.

Home isn't anything other than a person giving you a reason to stay.

When someone tells you the worst thing that has ever happened, I dare you not to fall in love with them.

Love comes unplanned, tapping on your shoulder whispering, "I'm about to fuck up your life in the best way."

The measure of a person's character is defined by how they choose to exit your story.

If you are proud of the person you are, it's your past mistakes that made you that way.

I challenge you to let go of everyone and only reach again to those few people who are still hanging on for dear life refusing to let you go.

If you want to know a girl's story, find the song that makes her cry. Listen to it and ask her about her past.

If you are good to them I promise you, darling, they will miss you.

My mom always said, "Kill them with kindness." Be so kind that if someone doesn't like you everyone else thinks they are crazy for it.

While some people mean everything they say, others master the art of deception, using words as weapons to destroy you.

Be wary of whom you bring to the top with you; some people reach for your hand only to bring you down.

Sometimes the one person you never thought would hurt you is the one that brings you to your knees. And sometimes the person you never expected is the one that picks you up again.

Don't let history trick you into thinking there is going to be a future.

The question should never be why is someone leaving but rather why are you wasting time caring about someone who doesn't want to stay.

And when someone leaves, let them go without a chase. Allow them to figure out what they need to. And trust once they find those answers they are looking for, they'll come back.

One of the hardest things in life is to watch someone you love self-destruct knowing well you could do nothing but pick up the pieces when it's over.

When you find what makes you happy, you owe it to yourself to always go back.

To fully love meant to surrender parts of you and give away pieces of yourself in the process.

Darling, you've loved every wrong person with everything you had. Imagine what it'll be like when you get it right.

There is something quite inviting about a vile poison that you suspect may kill you. There is something enticing about danger and taking chances and playing with fire just to get burned.

Sometimes happy endings consist of a heartbreaking goodbye that doesn't leave you bitter, but rather happy to have known another person in the first place.

Chapters ending are never easy, especially when it is with someone you thought would be at the end of the book.

And maybe the only reason you're running as much as you are is in hope you turn back around and find that someone cares enough to chase you.

Let them fall in love with your breakdowns and smeared makeup and drunk confessions and honesty. Let them fall in love with all you are and accept you for all you aren't.

But the greatest company ever is that in which you "want" to be alone, because that's never really the case. Even in our isolation and a state of pushing people away, all we really want is someone who stays.

Love does not discriminate against labels. It does not ask, "Are you guys official yet?" It does not ask, "Is this a bad time?" or "Is he the right person?" Love chooses us, and no matter how much we'd like to deny it, and the more we do, love does not tell a lie. And once your heart chooses, you are at its whim and under its complete control.

There's something that draws you in about the Devil. And with every devil comes an angel. Because maybe you need him. Maybe you thrive on the drama. Just maybe you need him as much as he needs you.

But love isn't this. Love isn't this adrenaline rush of emotions. Love isn't tearing someone apart. Love isn't pain. Love isn't confusion. Love doesn't leave you wondering. Love isn't trying so hard to keep someone's attention. Love is simple. Love is supposed to build you up and not knock you down. Love is supposed to fill you and not leave you empty as you sacrifice parts of yourself to appease them.

So you throw back a shot because even the most bitter of alcohol tastes better than salty tears.

To lose oneself to another person is life's greatest tragedy.

"I love yous" aren't words you can take back. Once they are said, it's like they are written in concrete, dried within the heart of the other person forever.

There are those types of people who know pain at such an extreme level that average people won't ever understand them. Those people are like art. They are made from smeared paint and complete chaos, making up something too beautiful for words.

So run, my dear. Run as far and fast as you can. When you get far enough, the ghost that will haunt you most when you look back will be regret.

Remember, it's a lonely road to the top when all you've ever done is step on people like me to get there.

You overthink because you care.
You worry because you don't want to ever hurt anyone.
You question yourself because people have led you to believe it's you that is flawed.
But darling, you should know your heart isn't like the rest of them.
You were made to feel a little more.
You were made to care a little more.
Sadly, that means you're gonna get hurt a little more.
But keep being you.
Keep doing your best.
Because it is enough. You are enough.

There is a time for silence. A time where being quiet will speak louder than any words can. Sometimes there aren't words for pain. Sometimes there aren't words for disappointment. Sometimes you have to let silence do its work.

I see you are hurting.
And I want it to go away.
I see you are beautiful.
Even though I know you've cried a lot lately.
And I can't make it stop.
Or heal your heart.
But what I can tell you is you're not alone, even if it feels like you are right now.

Have you ever stood in a crowded room and felt like the loneliest person there?

The most important thing isn't wanting someone to wake up and realize you're it after all this time. The most important thing is meeting someone who realizes it right then and there in no time at all.

One of the hardest things you'll ever do is walk away from someone you love, admitting that love in itself wasn't enough to save you.

I think your problem, dear, is you want to be loved, yet you won't let anyone close enough to love you. I think your problem, dear, is you want to love someone but you won't let anyone in.

You're dating the man of our dreams. Take care of him.

When someone matters, distance is merely a mathematical complication of your mind.

I didn't know how to save you from yourself.

Don't open doors that took so long to close.

Sometimes rock bottom is life's most solid platform to build on.

He

He saved me by teaching me I could save myself.

And even if I were to fuck up my entire life, he'd still be standing next to me saying, "Okay, what's our next move and how can we make this better?" It's the type of loyalty everyone dreams of.

I asked for a long explanation and all he said was, "I'm choosing to be here because I want to be."

He told me he was proud of me and I asked why. And he said, "Because I can see it across your face how hurt you are right now, but you aren't staying down."

He said he'd call me right back. That was the last I ever heard of him. And even though years have passed, if he called back I'd still answer.

At the end of the day what it came down to was when my world felt it was crashing and burning, he'd come anywhere, anytime, and save me every time. It was a loyalty unlike anything I've ever known.

They. Always. Come. Back.

You broke her heart and she was the one to apologize. Let that sink in for a moment.

I really couldn't find more elegant words to say other than, "Thank you." He kept a fire alive within me for so long, and even in his absence, he lived never to be forgotten.

"I'm happy for you," appeared across my screen, and that's when I knew it was over. In a storm I'd learned to dance through, I knew I made it. But even four words broke me a little. Maybe it was for the past, soon to be forgotten. Maybe it was for a future that would never be. Or maybe it was because he was my favorite person to dance with in the rain.

He taught me a lot of things. Above all was that I could make a million mistakes, say all the wrong things, humiliate myself over and over again, call too many times, triple text, and at the end of the day he was there every time. He still looked at me and said there isn't a thing you can say or do that could change how highly I view you or the respect I have for you. That's what I hoped for in every person I met but knew how rare it was to find.

He saw me in a world in which I tried to be invisible, only to whisper, "You never were. Everyone has seen you, but your head's been down this whole time."

He kissed my forehead, leaving an invisible mark that would send shivers through my soul and a feeling of always longing for more.

There was something about him that was different. Just standing in his vicinity, even in silence, made me a better person. I don't know how many people have the ability to do something like that.

The only thing scarier than being with her would be not being with her and knowing someone like her exists in the world and he did nothing about it.

Some would argue they were a terrible influence on each other, but their flaws complemented one another in such a way that whatever one was lacking, the other made up for.

His heart ached at her memory, thinking back to all they were. He knew she loved him more than anyone on the planet. But he couldn't be what she needed.

He was never meant to stay. And every time he left, she took a big enough piece of him with her that he had to come back for it.

She pushed everyone away except him. He never let her. Because every time she tried he'd pull her in, hold her tight, and whisper, "Not me, too. I'm here to stay."

It wasn't even a first love. He was simply an extension of myself. We grew in different directions but so much of whom I was, was because of him. He was embedded within me. If you stripped me of all I was and I stood bare, you would see him underneath it.

He took my hand, asking me to dance in the middle of the night on a bridge with white lights as he sang my favorite song. If that wasn't a real-life fairy tale I don't know what was. But it was the type of night that ruined me in the best way because I knew looking at him that fairy tales could be real.

He asked me if I'd ever be willing to have his kids. I ran my fingers through his hair and thought there wouldn't be a greater privilege in my life.

Fathers play the most important role in a daughter's life. They show through example what she deserves in a man. He'll hand off the baton to the man most worthy, and it'll be the happiest/saddest day of his life.

"You still love me?"
"Yes."
"How do you know?"
"Because I don't hate you after all you put me through."

But there was something different in him that night. Maybe it was the look in his eyes. Maybe it was him pulling away when I reached for his hand. Maybe it was in the goodbye, where he held me a little tighter, allowing me to be the one to let go. I think he foresaw my future in those coming months when I was blind to it.

And with your arms around me in the pouring rain, I whispered, "I love you." And you held me tighter not letting go, as you replied, "I know." The rain mixed with tears you never saw.

If there was any person on this earth who could love and treat him as well as I could, it was her. And I found comfort in knowing they found each other. I found comfort in knowing he'd be taken care of. So I walked away and sometimes I wondered if she knew. But there was a respect between us. A love I had for her, too, because she was everything he deserved and then some.

You're a devil who charmed me as you took my hand asking for just one dance.

The only thing that kept him here was the thought of her weeping at his casket. He could hurt others, but not her. The thought of hurting her gave him enough strength to stay. He knew one day he'd have to thank her for that.

They loved each other. Not enough to be together, but enough that they couldn't walk away.

He could feel her letting go; with every word she spoke she sounded so distant. And he found himself reaching for her more often than before. Although he never said it, he didn't want her to go. It was in these moments he finally understood what she felt like every time he walked away.

"I know it hurts to let go..." he began. She cut him off with tears in her eyes. "No. Living without you hurts. Losing you, that would hurt. But letting go of something that is toxic for me doesn't hurt compared to the first two."

He wanted to know he mattered, so I wrote a book about him.

She

She was the type who when she hit rock bottom it was never gracefully but rather violently and fast to a point where she broke to pieces at the bottom. But she never stayed down long. That was key.

She knows how you feel. What she doesn't know is why you're not doing anything about it.

She said goodbye with tears in her eyes not because she didn't love him. But she knew love wasn't supposed to hurt you this much.

And that was the thing about her: if at any moment you wanted to come back into her life, she'd welcome you with open arms and give you a chance to prove she was right about you this whole time.

She knew how you treated her said more about you than it ever did about her.

She wasn't like the rest of them. It was both a blessing and a curse.

She kissed his cheek and said goodbye for what she knew would be a final time. And that was the beauty and tragedy of it, really: getting what you want, only to run away when it got too close.

Don't be a coward. Go up. Kiss her. Take her hand. And walk away. The end.

She was caught somewhere between missing him and respecting herself enough not to show it.

And in a crowded room full of hundreds, even if every eye were on her, she'd still only have eyes for him. She saw through everyone and everything. Because in a crowded room it was only him that mattered.

I didn't say anything, but I think she understood. She saw something in my eyes maybe and just knew. It was only a moment or two, but I'll always remember her for that.

She deserves more than waiting and you deserve someone you're more sure of.

She missed him. And she knew it'd pass and she'd get over him. But right now in this moment, she was allowed to miss him. She was allowed to feel through this thing until it passed.

Her beauty she kept quietly hidden, revealed in small bits enough to make them fall to their knees and always come back for more.

To love deeply in a world where she only knew heartbreak was life's greatest accomplishment.

She was completely captivated by complexity, welcoming trouble with a coy smile, eager to learn about the scars that told stories too beautiful for words.

Sometimes we crave the touch of someone holding us so tight that all our broken pieces just stay in place for a moment.

She compiled a draft of what she wanted in another soul. When the Devil found it he morphed into this image, using it to later destroy her.

It was his disbelief in love that gave her something to want to prove.

She touched him feeling every bit of imperfection, finally finding a place that felt like home.

She taught me we get this one life to live, one life to fuck up a bit, and one love to find happiness and love while doing so.

Despite her insanity she was lovely.

Her walls came crumbling down with his touch and suddenly he knew why the world's most beautiful structures were always behind walls with guards.

She was unapologetically herself even when it made her look bad.

Be the example that makes her question everyone else in her past but never you.

It takes a special kind of person to love someone who is broken. Because it isn't simply loving them. It's teaching them everything they've come to believe and being the exception. It's teaching them they can trust someone other than themselves. In return, they'll doubt you. They'll question you and second-guess everything. They'll want more than anything to run the other way. Don't let them. Because once they trust you, they'll love you harder than you thought anyone could. They will redefine what you thought love even meant. And you'll never be the same again.

She believed everyone had the potential to be good when given enough chances.

She didn't care about what others thought of him. She cared about the way his presence in a room made her heart flutter the way only roller coasters dropping could.

You could see her eyes light up as she spoke about the things she loved. And he'd spend the rest of his life hoping to love something to that extent. But the only thing that ever came close was her.

She wasn't afraid of asking pressing questions. She knew the only way to really know someone was to look them in the eyes and ask about the things they regret. And with a simple look she'd see through men and they'd tell her everything.

She looked at him in a way children look at something they see for the first time with wide eyes and a vision of perfection.

She was the sun and he the moon. She light and he darkness. But they needed each other the way the oceans need the shore to violently crash into but be beautiful.

She wasn't meant to be healed or have her broken pieces put back together. She just needed someone to run their fingers around her rough edges and say I love you.

She said, "Please leave so I know what it's like to live without you."

He turned to her and said, "I'd never want to know such a life. More so, I'm selfish and I'd like to keep you if you let me."

The most beautiful part about her was she taught him to accept the past he tried so hard to run from.

Everyone questioned her judgment. Despite that, she looked at him with complete confidence. Whom he became, in the end, was proof of how spot-on she was about people. He taught her to trust herself more and in return there was this loyalty between them. Because even when he wasn't that person yet, she never stopped believing he would be.

She reached for everyone else hoping that maybe saving someone would help her save herself.

She loved him and he knew. He knew it every time he hurt her. He knew it every time he disappointed her. He knew it every time he walked away. But he'd look at her across the room and she'd look back smiling, hiding the pain. But the thing was he hurt, too. He hurt knowing he broke the heart of someone who would never do the same.

Her greatest flaw is that she runs from anything good that gets close to her, right into the arms of the person that made her that way.

She hung on as long as she could. Against all odds. Against all doubts. She held on for dear life. He couldn't help but respect her for that. And he knew she never would let go. So he had to be the one to let go, for her own sake and sanity. He knew she deserved someone who could give her something he couldn't. Someone to love her the way she loved him. And there were moments he wanted to be that person, but in his heart of hearts, he knew she deserved so much more.

They didn't understand him and that's what she liked about it; she liked knowing something they didn't.

People come into our lives for all sorts of reasons, just as people sometimes inexplicably exit our lives. Sometimes, they leave with goodbyes; other times, they are taken from us for no rhyme or reason. They act as comets in the night sky, lighting up our worlds before disappearing into the darkness.

Death is so difficult because it comes bearing acceptance without understanding.

Her words were beautiful. Her mind, though, must have been a place full of hell.

Friendship isn't a contract signed in stone, but rather someone standing in front of a door that is open.

Sometimes love isn't enough to change waking up in a bed too big for one.

It takes great courage to love and greater courage to walk away knowing when it's served its purpose.

It's beautifully ironic and yet understandable that those who do not believe in love experienced it at its deepest level.

They fell in love with one another just as you do songs: first rejecting the unfamiliar, then suddenly every word was on repeat.

Always stay honest in a world full of liars.

Unfortunately, we don't choose whom we love.

The hardest part wasn't seeing each of us accomplish everything we once talked about. The hardest part was accepting we were able to do it without each other. But there wasn't a silent fan cheering you on any louder.

We could have been something great. But could haves, should haves, and maybes only kept me up at night tossing and turning.

Sometimes we pour salt on old wounds just to see if it'll hurt...one day I promise you it will stop hurting.

Ironically the loudest sound in the entire world is the silence of a cell phone when we don't want it to be.

It broke me a bit because we were both good people with the best intentions, but after a while, we just stopped being good for each other.

We have two choices. We can either keep getting hurt or we can ask ourselves why and try to change it.

We focus so much on the wrong people that sometimes we fail to see the right one was right in front of us if we opened our eyes and looked.

As I looked you in the eyes, I saw the cold look of a stranger and I knew all we had in common was the past we wanted to forget.

We are all compiled of broken pieces for a reason. And as we interact we trade these pieces with one another to make another person whole. We are beautifully broken but always whole, filled with bits and pieces of everyone we've ever known and will come to know in the future.

*"We were like free birds with broken wings because
we had nowhere to fly."*
—Eva Gutman (Holocaust survivor and friend)

We are all destined to destroy each other in the end.

We are defined in the moments that are meant to break us.

Sometimes in an attempt to restore something that is broken, our fingers get cut in the process.

Let's get a little lost in the towns we don't know and find ourselves along the way.

Our insecurities kill us like a vile poison we fed to ourselves.

At one point in time, we will all become those people we swore we'd never be.

We are who we are; nothing more, nothing less.

I don't think we're scared of things working out. Quite the contrary, we are all scared shitless of something going right.

We're all addicts in different forms, set on getting high with different things. I didn't need you. I wanted you. I wanted you the way addicts want the same drugs that kill them.

The moment we touched I was forever tainted with everything you were and more than accepting of everything you weren't.

Our spirits were connected, souls intertwined and with that, I knew we'd meet again.

There was once a time we were writing this story together, and somewhere along the way he wrote a sequel, forgetting to add me in as one of the main characters.

Of the greatest robbers in life is time, as are we for thinking we will never run out of it.

But you aren't alone, dear. We're all runners looking for someone who gives us a reason to stop.

And maybe we'll see each other again in another lifetime. When we're the people we need to be, instead of the false younger versions of what we wanted so badly to be, too soon. And maybe I'll see you at the end of the altar, where I can whisper the words, "I told you so."

We ended the same way we started, as strangers. Only this time, I had no desire to want to know you.

We liked that each of us was broken in our own ways. It was like we weren't alone in those moments we wanted to be. Because everyone knows, the greatest company comes when you don't want any. So in our states of loneliness, where we pushed everyone away, we still always let the other one join us in our isolation.

Because people like us were never meant to find each other. We were meant to think we were alone in this routine we call life. And now that we've found each other, we know we aren't the only crazy ones out there. We know there's at least one person as mad as we are.

We both know it wasn't supposed to end this way.

We are all a little broken, and maybe that's the beauty of it.

We were soul mates meant for a lifetime different than this. So for now, our shadows would delicately dance with one another until they became one and just maybe we'd find each other again in a life where we could find our forever.

The toughest goodbyes are never said nor understood.

I

I think if we stopped fucking with each other we'd realize how good this thing could actually be.

I didn't want to have to question if someone cares about me. That's too tiring. I just wanted to look at someone and know with complete confidence.

At that moment something really good happened; you were the first I wanted to tell.

I'll be the first to admit I jump really quickly into things. And it might be a mistake. But I take these chances holding onto blind faith that this time instead of falling, just maybe I'll fly.

He was every dream she ever had.

Someone once asked me if I ever cheated. I never wanted to be the reason someone disbelieves in love.

One night with him was enough to make her want something more than everything she'd come to know. One night with him and she saw a future in his eyes.

Most of all I'm afraid of forgetting you. Maybe that's why I've been holding on so tight.

And maybe one day I'd be the person you deserved. But right now I'm a sinking ship and every time you tried to save me I was drowning you.

More than anything I missed who I wanted you to be. I missed believing you could be him.

I don't think I'm scared of things going wrong. I'm scared shitless of things going right, then suddenly having something to lose.

I think part of me would always miss you, even in those times you were standing right next to me.

I can't stop every bit of pain you feel. I can't write every story or say we've had the same experiences. There are some things I may never know and things that will live with you the rest of your life. But what I can tell you is you are not alone in anything you are going through. I'm with you.

I want you to think of the worst day of your entire life; now I want you to keep going because you got through it.

I'd risk a sleepless night if it meant talking to you the whole time.

Today my mom asked me what happened.
And my heart broke all over again when I replied, "I don't know."
She then asked if it hurt as bad as the last time.
All I could say was, "Pain is pain."

You were never mine, but I think part of me would always miss you like you were.

I will always hope it's us in the end.

Everyone always tells me to walk away. But I can never seem to. I'd rather take one more chance at the risk of blowing my heart to shreds than ever wonder what if.

I gave you time to think, and now your time is up. Because I never needed to think twice about you.

After a while I become so numb to it all, nothing ever hurt. I couldn't tell if that was a good thing or bad.

"It's scary," I said.
"The best things in life usually are."

I loved him a little more than I loved myself at the time. I think that's why it hurt so much to lose him.

I knew you weren't the only one, but it kind of felt like you were. Because in a world full of 7.4 billion people in each of them I looked for you. Maybe then I'd find myself.

I couldn't hate him because once I was in his shoes I realized how much easier it was to say, "I'm busy" than "I'm not interested."

And in the eyes of everyone that came after I looked for you in a desperate attempt to find myself once more.

I wasn't supposed to fall in love with you and you weren't supposed to break my heart.

The words "I love you" mistakenly slipped out of my mouth, and before I could take them back they were yours to have and I was all but consumed by you.

I didn't want better; I wanted you and only you.

And maybe I was attracted to things I knew I could never have. It captivated me completely, the yearning for something and always getting so close before it disappeared.

I could have and would have given you the world, knowing well that wouldn't have been enough to make you stay. But hell, I tried.

My heart broke more looking into your eyes. I was hoping something, anything would click and you'd remember. But all I saw was the cold look of a stranger I had once known.

I trusted imperfection.

I was captivated by the storms that came bearing destruction and left quietly, leaving broken pieces that would define history.

I wanted to say only one word if given the chance, "Sorry." But all I could come up with was a silence I let kill me.

I saw him in everything I looked at with regret.

And even if I knew it would end with unhappily ever after, I'd do it all again in a broken heartbeat.

I loved you in a way I knew you could never love me back the way I needed. That was either selfless courage or stupidity.

I knew I loved you in the moment I realized I could in fact live without you but I'd never want to do such a thing.

I was scared, but it was the type of fear where I knew I was doing something right.

When I ran through fire I never stopped when it got hot. I ran through the flames taking pride in the scars that prevailed.

I didn't trust people who didn't drink. I didn't trust people who didn't trust themselves in the art of completely falling apart with the help of alcohol. But most of all I didn't trust people until they saw me at my worst and woke up still liking me.

Even if I had much to say to you I'd rather choke on my words in silence than allow myself to be vulnerable.

I always just wanted to write something well enough that it would reach you, even if you were worlds away and you'd find your way back to me.

I was prepared for you to walk away so much, I held the door open until my arm hurt because I realized you didn't move.

I was drunk on love and a fool for believing slurred words.

Kindness was all I could offer and if that wasn't enough then I wasn't enough. But I wasn't going to apologize for it.

I didn't need someone to want me as much as I wanted someone to need me in such a way that their life without me would rob them of their sleep.

I didn't fear being alone as much as I feared holding the hand of a stranger.

There was something I found beautiful in smeared makeup and falling to my knees crying at 2 AM.

I knew I was ready to turn the page the moment you reached for me and my heart didn't skip a beat.

I hope my memory haunts you in your sleep and you wake up in a cold sweat as I meet you in your dreams.

It was the kind of kiss that ruined me for anyone in my future.

If loving him was wrong, then the last thing I wanted to be was right.

I don't know what day I fear more: your wedding day or mine.

I loved you without knowing when or why or how to make it stop.

I was laughing at jokes I hadn't fully heard. Physically, I was there but mentally and emotionally I left my heart with him.

I swore I was looking for love but in reality, I was running from it.

It was like watching a train wreck in slow motion that wasn't about to crash just yet. And I stayed put, glued to the images I didn't want to be real, but I knew it was coming. The short conversations with words that hung were consumed by awkward silences. The goodbyes left me wondering if there'd be another hello. I suddenly was censoring what was coming out of my mouth, because "I love you" stings with the response, "I know."

But I fall in love with broken people. I fall in love with imperfection. I fall in love with stories of the past that bring tears to people's eyes. I love the look in someone's eyes when they're talking about something they really love. I love the excitement in their voice when something good happens. But I also love the bad stuff. I love the breakdowns, the tears, and the high intensity of emotions. I love that moment when they trust you enough to tell you the worst thing that's ever happened to them.

I tried to find myself at the bottom of the bottle and all I found when I got there was how much I still loved you.

And the only arms I ran to were the same ones that caused me to become this person I no longer recognized. That's what an addiction is—trying to find comfort in the same thing that destroys you.

I stood there 3,000 miles away. I realized home wasn't a place. Home was him and I was finally ready to stop running.

I know you look at your parents and question love and relationships. My hope is we get it right the way they never did.

I was never whole in the first place. Then I met him and I realized why.

It was like I was playing the main character in someone else's life. I looked at my reflection and saw a stranger.

I've always been wary of enemies, but I never thought I'd have to be wary of my own best friend.

And with tears in my eyes, I looked up at him and said, "I'm sorry but I've fallen in love with you. I think you are one of the most extraordinary people I've ever known."

I couldn't hate her. I wanted to. But I knew well enough that it takes the right woman to make a man out of a boy. And I'll admit she did something I wasn't able to. So more than hating her, I respected her for making him the man I always knew he would be.

And before I knew it, it was over. But you didn't bother to ask me if my heart was ready for that sort of thing yet.

When you looked into my eyes I knew you saw someone else. It's one of those things you can't hide from girls ever.

I always tell people who are hurt that two things will happen. Either the person who hurt you will come back, realizing the mistake they made, or you move on and meet someone even better. I think both scenarios are all too promising, so I ask you to hold onto that.

And if there's ever a day we look at each other and I'm not overcome with regret and sorrow, it'll be a day too soon.

It hurt to let go. But it hurt more holding onto something that wasn't there anymore.

It was only after he left that I realized how much I loved him. And I kept it a secret for so long. But the pain I felt in his absence made me realize I never loved someone so deeply.

I was gonna be whatever he needed me to be. If he wanted to love me I already loved him. If he wanted to be my friend I'd take a bullet for him. If he wanted me to be a stranger I'd break my heart to look at him and pretend we didn't know each other at all. But I wanted him happy even if it meant without me.

Love is hell; I just didn't think I'd find this hell looking into such beautiful blue eyes that saw right through me.

The recovering drug addict: a statistic no one keeps track of. It's a statistic of the person who survived. And while many will judge you for a past you regret, I'm just proud you made it.

Because I would have accepted all your darkness. I loved your rough edges even though mine weren't. I loved you for your past because I thought I saw something in what could be our future.

Because somewhere between clothes on the floor and your fingers running through my hair, I thought this was different.

He looked at me uttering words that broke my heart, "I can't give you what you deserve. I can't be what you need. I want you to find someone who can." Years would pass and I wish I could have thanked him for that instead of having cursed him off.

Dear Daddy on my Wedding Day: While it seems like you are losing me to the love of my life. Always remember I loved you first.

My dad once told me you don't think things through, you just do them.

I replied, "You're right. I don't think. I feel. And if it feels right that's what I follow. And I've never regretted it. Not once."

Part of me will always miss you. Part of me missed you even when you were a foot in front of me. Because even with arms wrapped around me as we lay in the same bed I always felt like we were miles apart and the inevitable was you leaving.

And you might be a demon and I might be the first to dance with you and maybe we're dancing in a place called hell but you should know this also happens to be my playground.

I don't want to know a story or accept one where it isn't us at the end of all of this.

With him, conflicts between my heart and head appeared like a boxing match.

"Goodbye" seems like a foreign word that was exchanged between others, not us. And you haven't said it yet, but I can feel it that you don't want to be here anymore.

I fall to my knees and I cry on the bathroom floor because I can feel you letting go. I feel it in my bones you aren't with me like you used to be. Where you were once the person I turned to for everything, I find myself lonely. I find myself enduring this and I reach for you and you aren't reaching back. My stomach hurts, my face is sweating, tears trickle down. I find myself throwing up with a fever. I didn't know someone's absence could affect another human they way you have me. But I'm hurting. It's almost like I'm coming up for air but it's being denied to me. That's what it feels like being without you.

From our first kiss, I knew I wanted him to be my last.

There's always been a fire in my heart that burns bright. I need someone who adds fuel to it. I need someone who can walk with me through flames and not be afraid of getting burned. I need someone who will exchange intense looks and without words know what I'm saying. I need someone who understands the parts of myself I'm still afraid of.

I love you enough to hate you. Because hell, that's my only chance I have at overcoming you.

It was only two weeks, but he taught me time means nothing. Part of me would love him even a little bit for that.

I was jumping through hoops of fire trying to get you to notice me. I didn't realize the self-destruction I caused every time I got burned.

I've come to learn the things and people we fear losing most usually get lost in time and even when we see it coming, there's no way to prepare for the flood of emotions like a tsunami that come our way when our fears become reality.

The best/worst day of my life will be when I introduce you to him. I don't know who he is yet, but when I meet someone good enough and that day comes, you'll know that's it. He replied, "I look forward to that day because you deserve it."

I was still fumbling for words to describe what had happened between us. And when people ask how you are, I pretend I know. It's easier to lie than explain how we got here. 'Cause I still don't know and I still find myself hoping we'll go back.

I sit here pen to paper struggling to articulate everything. In a life where I've made a career out of words, I can't come up with much other than, "Thank you."

I kept my phone on every night anticipating his call. And as 3 AM came I'd wake up to his ringtone. He'd take me to these dark places in his mind. Fearlessly, I took his hand and was led to the depths of hell. While a lot of it I couldn't understand, what I did know was that if he was on the phone with me, he was with us. And if he was with us he was safe.

In the coming years, he thanked me.

I never told him that saving him saved me in a way, because learning about him taught me about myself. Learning about him taught me about the person I didn't want to be. From there, I chose a different path. I chose to use words to save people from themselves.

It's 2:30 AM. And if you're awake you might be overthinking something. And if you are awake you might be lonely. It's 3:00 AM and I'm sure some of you question where you are going and why you should even bother. It's 3:30 AM and I'm sure dark thoughts have danced in your mind and you wish they'd go away. It's 4:00 AM and I'm asking you that instead of making any rash decisions right now, close your eyes, go back to sleep, and try again tomorrow.

He saved my life in a way, and I never really got to thank him for that. Because how do you even convey that in words? So I sat there in silence riding shotgun in his car years later and if silence could speak it would have said thank you.

Dedicated to anyone who has ever lost someone to suicide or to those beautiful fragile souls who have chosen to stay.

Darling. I need you here. Please don't go so soon.

KIRSTEN CORLEY is a writer born and raised in New Jersey who currently resides in Brooklyn. Her passions include writing about relationships and helping people understand the things they are going through. She uses her own life experience as the focal point for her work to really connect with readers on a deep, emotional level. When she isn't writing, she's an advocate for causes at Covenant House for homeless youth, suicide, and mental health awareness and volunteers with those who are mentally handicapped while being a mentor for Big Brothers and Big Sisters. A former college volleyball player (at Stockton University) turned distance runner, she has run 13 half marathons and 2 full marathons.

**THOUGHT
CATALOG
Books**

Thought Catalog Books is a publishing house owned by The Thought & Expression Company, an independent media group based in Brooklyn, NY. Founded in 2010, we are committed to facilitating thought and expression. We exist to help people become better communicators and listeners in order to engender a more exciting, attentive, and imaginative world. For general information and submissions: hello@thoughtcatalog.com. Visit us on the web at www.thought.is or www.thoughtcatalog.com.

ISBN 978-1-945796-17-3
10 9 8 7 6 5 4 3 2

Printed and bound in the United States of America.

Made in the USA
Monee, IL
29 November 2019